A LIGHT LUNCH

A R Gurney

BROADWAY PLAY PUBLISHING INC
New York
www.broadwayplaypublishing.com
info@broadwayplaypublishing.com

A LIGHT LUNCH
© Copyright 2009 A R Gurney

Cover art by David Prittie
First printing: March 2009
I S B N: 978-0-88145-438-3
Book design: Marie Donovan
Word processing: Microsoft Word
Typographic controls: Ventura Publisher
Typeface: Palatino
Printed and bound in the U S A

The world premiere of A LIGHT LUNCH was by
The Flea Theater (Jim Simpson, Artistic Director; Carol
Ostrow, Producing Director), with the first performance
on 12 December 2008. The cast and creative
contributors were:

BETH . . . . .Beth Hoyt
VIOLA . . . . Havilah Brewster
GARY . . . . .Tom Lipinski
MARSHALL . . . . .John Russo

Director . . . . Jim Simpson
Set design . . . . .John McDermott
Lighting design . . . . .Miranda Hardy
Sound design . . . . .Jill B C DuBoff
Costume design . . . . Erin Murphy
Stage manager . . . . Shani Murfin
Assistant director. . . . . .Courtney Wetzel
Props design . . . . Michael Guagno
Caricatures . . . . .Paul Howard
Press . . . . .Ron Lasko/Spin Cycle

CHARACTERS & SETTING

BETH
VIOLA
GARY
MARSHALL

all in their twenties

Set: A small table in a far corner of a low-key restaurant in the New York theater district. Other tables, set but unoccupied, may be nearby. On the walls, theater posters, caricatures of actors, or other memorabilia.

Time: Around noon

for everyone at the Flea Theater

(At rise:)

(BETH enters briskly. She is young lawyer, wearing a stylish suit, carrying a classy briefcase. She is followed by VIOLA, a young waitress, wearing an apron, holding a couple of well-used menus).

BETH: *(Surveying the area)* This will do.

VIOLA: You asked to be off in a corner.

BETH: We don't want to disturb other people.

VIOLA: And you don't want other people to disturb you.

BETH: Exactly.

VIOLA: May I ask...will this be a...well, a romantic meeting?

BETH: Oh no, no, no, no.

VIOLA: I could easily put fresh flowers on the table.

BETH: Don't bother. This is strictly a working lunch. All business, from the get-go.

VIOLA: Gotcha. *(Distributing menus)* I'm Viola, by the way. I'll be serving you today..

BETH: Hi Viola. *(Looking off)* Will there be people at those tables nearby?

VIOLA: Not these days.

BETH: Why not these days?

VIOLA: The recession and all.

BETH: Oh that.

VIOLA: More and more people are settling for sandwiches at their desks. If they still have desks.

BETH: Yes well, the reason I'm being a sticker is that we'll probably be tossing some familiar names around the infield, and I don't want strangers listening in.

VIOLA: Are you in the theatre?

BETH: No, no. I'm just a lowly lawyer. But I'll be meeting with a theatre person. About theatre things. He recommended this restaurant.

VIOLA: That's because theatre people come here all the time. Lauren Bacall ate a mushroom omelet here. Alec Baldwin sat where you're sitting now.

BETH: Oh well. We're hardly in that category....

VIOLA: I'm in show business myself.

BETH: Are you really?

VIOLA: Oh yes. I act. I wait to act. Get it?

BETH: I do. And your name is, again?

VIOLA: Viola.

BETH: Viola's a pretty name.

VIOLA: I took it from the character in *Twelfth Night*. I played her in high school.

BETH: Interesting.

VIOLA: My real name is Mildred, but I don't broadcast it. In high school they called me Mill-dewed.

BETH: Oh dear.

VIOLA: You can see why I had to change it.

BETH: I do, I do.

VIOLA: *(Reciting)* "I prithee, and I'll pay thee bounteously, Conceal me what I am, and be my aid..."

BETH: I won't tell a soul, Viola. But since you're an actress...

VIOLA: A*ctor*. Actresses are actors now.

BETH: All right. Since you're an actor, may I ask a quick question about the theatre?

VIOLA: Go ahead.

BETH: Have you ever heard of a playwright named Gurney?

VIOLA: Who?

BETH: Gurney.

VIOLA: Now wait. I'm thinking. I believe my boyfriend knows more about him. He teaches theater.

BETH: Gurney?

VIOLA: No, my boy friend.

BETH: What does he say about Gurney?

VIOLA: Let's see. Gurney. Hmmm. Is he the one who's been around like forever?

BETH: I believe so. Yes.

VIOLA: And he writes plays about WASPs?

BETH: Apparently, yes.

VIOLA: But not just WASPs. I think my boyfriend said that some of Gurney's plays now have Jewish people in them.

BETH: I should hope so.

VIOLA: Is Gurney the person you're meeting with today?

BETH: Good God no. Just with his agent.

VIOLA: His agent? Oh hey! Does his agent handle actors?

BETH: That I wouldn't know.

VIOLA: Would you mind if I slipped my head-shot and resume into his dessert menu?

BETH: Up to you.

VIOLA: As Shakespeare says in *Twelfth Night*, "Some are born great, some achieve greatness, but agents have greatness thrust upon them."

BETH: Very good, Viola. *(Glancing off)* It's hard to see the door from here. Will you be keeping an eye out for him?

VIOLA: Oh sure. I'll do it now. *(Starts off)*

BETH: I have no idea what he looks like. We've only talked on the telephone.

VIOLA: No problem. I can spot an agent a mile away. *(She goes.)*

(BETH *takes out her Blackberry, dials.*)

BETH: *(Speaking into Blackberry)* Arrived in New York. All systems go. With luck, hope to catch the five-fifteen back, and report in first thing tomorrow morning... Bye" *(Closes Blackberry, takes out compact, puts on lipstick, combs her hair. Checks her watch. Opens her briefcase, takes out an impressive looking legal document, glances at it, puts it back. Picks up menu, glances nervously through it.)*

(VIOLA *returns with* GARY, *who is youngish, wears a jacket with jeans.)*

VIOLA: *(A la a T V host)* And now here's... *(To* GARY) What's your name again?

GARY: Gary.

VIOLA: This is Gary.

(BETH *stands up.)*

GARY: Am I late?

BETH: I was early. ...I'm Beth.

GARY: *(They shake hands.)* Hiya, Beth...

BETH: Hi, Gary.

VIOLA: I'm Viola.

(BETH and GARY look at VIOLA.)

VIOLA: I'll be your server today.

GARY: Hi, Viola.

BETH: Thank you, Viola.

VIOLA: Exit Viola.

(VIOLA goes; BETH and GARY sit at the table.)

GARY: Have a good flight?

BETH: What a question! No flights are good these days. Especially all the way from Texas.

GARY: I assume you flew Business Class.

BETH: Why assume that?

GARY: A fancy lawyer? From a major Texas law firm?

BETH: I'm low on the totem pole. I'm just starting out.

GARY: I can identify with that.

BETH: I must say I expected an older man.

GARY: Why?

BETH: Isn't Mister Gurney old?

GARY: Ancient.

BETH: I assumed his agent would be old, too.

GARY: The older agents handle mainly musicals now. There's more money there. So they gave Gurney to me.

BETH: And Gurney writes only plays?

GARY: Only plays.

BETH: Don't you have other clients?

GARY: Most of them have switched to T V.

BETH: So you're a T V agent too?

GARY: I should be. Except I prefer plays.

BETH: Why is that?

GARY: You connect more with the writers when you handle their plays. You work with them. You help arrange productions. You influence the casting. You participate in the whole creative process....

BETH: Does that happen with Gurney?

GARY: Sometimes. Yes.

BETH: Sounds like fun.

GARY: I can't say I'm bringing in much money for the agency. I'm not sure how long I'll last.

BETH: Or how long Gurney will last?

GARY: That, too.

(VIOLA *enters.*)

VIOLA: Folks want something to drink?

BETH: Just water, please.

VIOLA: How about a glass of white wine?

BETH: *(To* GARY*)* Want one?

GARY: Maybe later, depending how things go.

VIOLA: We have a nice, dry Pinot Grigio.

BETH: You heard the gentleman, Viola. Just water, please.

VIOLA: Plain or bottled?

BETH: Ah well. *(To* GARY*)* What do you think?

VIOLA: The manager tells us to push bottled. *(Conspiratorially)* But our New York water is famous.

BETH: All right. Regular water.

VIOLA: How about a bottle of bubbly?

BETH: No thank you, Viola.

VIOLA: You might need it.

BETH: Why would we need it?

VIOLA: Because I sense you're cranking up for a big scene.

BETH: *(To GARY)* Viola's an actress.

VIOLA: Actor.

GARY: *(To BETH)* Half the waiters in New York are actors.

VIOLA: I always advise bubbly to theatre folks. It settles the stomach should a conflict arise....

BETH: Why do you think we'll have a conflict, Viola?

VIOLA: Oh the theatre thrives on conflict.

BETH: Oh dear.

GARY: On resolution, too, Viola.

BETH: *(Patiently to VIOLA)* Both kinds of water, please, Viola.

VIOLA: Both you shall have. *(She goes)*

BETH: Well, Gary. Shall we get started on our "big scene"?

GARY: You kick it off. You called the meeting.

BETH: Fair enough. As I told you on the phone, I want to option a play by Gurney.

GARY: That's always good news. At least for Gurney.

BETH: I should think so.

GARY: But you didn't mention a client.

BETH: Didn't I?

GARY: You did not. *(Pause)* Well?

BETH: Well what?

GARY: Who is he? Or she, I should add.

BETH: It's a he, actually.

GARY: And the name?

BETH: I doubt if you'd recognize it.

GARY: Someone from Texas?

BETH: That's right.

GARY: A Texas millionaire?

BETH: Yes. All right. Yes.

GARY: I'd like to know his name.

BETH: Actually, he prefers to remain anonymous.

GARY: Anonymous?

BETH: That's what he prefers.

GARY: Surely you don't expect—

(GARY stops as VIOLA returns with the a pitcher of ice water, she pours it slowly and carefully.)

VIOLA: Go right on. Don't mind me.

GARY: *(To BETH)* Maybe we'd better review the bidding here.

BETH: Good idea.

VIOLA: *(As she pours)* I love that expression, "review the bidding". It comes from the game of Bridge, doesn't it?

GARY: I guess it does.

VIOLA: You know what we call it in the theatre?

BETH: *(Impatiently)* What, Viola?

VIOLA: We call it exposition. That's what you're really doing.... *(To* GARY*)* Am I right? You're doing the exposition?

GARY: That we are, Viola.

VIOLA: So go right ahead. Do it. I'm used to working right on through it....

BETH: Trouble is, I'm not, Viola.

VIOLA: Oh. Sorry, sorry, sorry. *(She goes.)*

BETH: Did I hurt her feelings?

GARY: I doubt it.

BETH: I'm not nuts about her, frankly.

GARY: She's very New York.

BETH: Well let's go on with our —what is it again?

GARY: Exposition. O K. You call my agency from Texas. You say you want to speak to whoever represents Gurney. They give you me, and you tell me you want to fly up and talk about optioning one of Gurney's plays. So you ask me to pick a place where we can discuss it over a light lunch. And here we are.

BETH: Here we are. I like this place, by the way. Quiet and low-key. It's just right.

GARY: On the phone you didn't say your client wants to remain anonymous.

BETH: Didn't I?

GARY: Come on. You don't expect me to make a deal with a stranger.

BETH: I'm hoping we'll find ways of working things out....

GARY: Tell you what. Just for the hell of it, let's proceed blindly.

BETH: Good idea.

GARY: Let's start by naming the play.

BETH: What?

GARY: Which play of Gurney's does your client want to option?

BETH: Has Gurney written many plays?

GARY: Too many, according to some critics.

BETH: Oh. Well. My client is interested in the new one.

GARY: Which new one?

BETH: Isn't there a new one?

GARY: There's a recent one, recently produced.

BETH: Is there one more recent even than that?

GARY: There might be.

BETH: That's the one we want.

GARY: What?

BETH: We want the newest one.

GARY: Are you serious?

BETH: I am.

GARY: This one is so new that it hasn't even been released.

BETH: Good.

GARY: I can't help wondering how you heard about it.

BETH: Rumors, I suppose.

GARY: Rumors?

BETH: Aren't there always a lot of rumors in the theater? Gossip and stuff?

GARY: I didn't know they drifted all the way down to Texas.

BETH: In this case, they must have. Because my client has heard about it and wants to snap it up....

GARY: This is all very strange. The play hasn't been submitted to a single soul.

BETH: That makes it all the more exciting....

GARY: Do you have any specifics in mind?

BETH: Specifics?

GARY: A director? Or actors? Or a particular space?

BETH: Not yet.

GARY: But your client is a producer?

BETH: Not really. No.

GARY: No? Then why in God's name should Gurney have anything to do with him?

BETH: Because he's a huge fan of Gurney's work..

GARY: Oh yes?

BETH: Huge! He recognizes Gurney's talent and he wants to...well, he wants to be actively involved in the creative process from the bottom up....

(VIOLA returns, providing glasses for the bubbly.)

VIOLA: Now for the bubbly. *(As she pours carefully from the bubbly bottle.)* "With beaded bubbles winking at the brim..." *(To GARY)* That's from *To A Nightingale* by John Keats. I do readings in the New York Public School Poetry program.

GARY: Thanks, Viola.

VIOLA: You're welcome. *(She continues to pour slowly and carefully.)* Have you finished your exposition?

GARY: Not quite, Viola.

VIOLA: Are you talking about a production?

GARY: We're not there yet.

VIOLA: When you get there, would there be something in it for me?

BETH: That's not on our agenda, Viola.

VIOLA: Just remember I may be working in a restaurant, but I'm what you agents call "technically available." *(She goes)*

BETH: She's quite intrusive, isn't she?

GARY: New York, New York.

BETH: Do you think I'd hurt her feelings if I told her to shut the hell up?

GARY: It would. Yes. So let's get back to the play.

BETH: Ah yes. The play.

(VIOLA comes in, with her notepad.)

VIOLA: Folks ready to order?

BETH: A few more minutes, please, Viola. We haven't had a chance to look at the menu.

VIOLA: I totally understand.

GARY: You might delay your entrance, Viola, till I give you a hand cue.

VIOLA: Gotcha... *(She goes.)*

BETH: She irritates the pants off me.

GARY: I get a kick out of her.

BETH: Let's talk about that play..

GARY: Gurney wouldn't want me to.

BETH: Is Gurney very secretive?

GARY: On this one, he is.

BETH: At least tell me one thing.

GARY: Depends what it is.

BETH: Why hasn't he released it?

GARY: It doesn't have an ending.

BETH: What do you mean?

GARY: Gurney says every play worth its salt should have some sort of an ending, and this new play has none.

BETH: So is he working on one?

GARY: Even as we speak.

BETH: We still want to option it.

GARY: Without an ending?

BETH: Without an ending.

GARY: Gurney will say no.

BETH: You're sure?

GARY: I don't even need to call him.

BETH: Suppose I gave him a good reason to change his mind....

GARY: And what would that be?

BETH: Money.

GARY: Money?

BETH: Texas money.

GARY: How much?

BETH: Depends what you tell me about the play. I want to make sure we're talking about the same thing. *(Opening her briefcase)* Or haven't you read it?

GARY: Of course I've read it. In fact, I'm the only person in the world who has.

BETH: Did you like it?

GARY: Very much.

BETH: You have to say that, don't you? As his agent...

GARY: A good agent knows a good play.

BETH: And this is a good one?

GARY: This one is...how shall I say? ...Sensational...

BETH: And no one else in your agency has read it?

GARY: Not a soul...

BETH: But you think it has possibilities.

GARY: Ultimate possibilities.

BETH: Even without an ending?

GARY: I'm sure Gurney will come up with a good one.

BETH: You're just being a good agent.

GARY: Thank you.

(GARY *signals off.* VIOLA *comes in.*)

VIOLA: Ready to order?

GARY: *(To* BETH*))* We should at least eat. Even if we're not getting anywhere.

BETH: I suppose....

(BETH *and* GARY *look at their menus.*)

VIOLA: Would you like to hear the specials?

BETH: No thank you.

VIOLA: You're sure? I'm very good at reciting them. Nathan Lane was here last week and he said I made the meat loaf sound absolutely delicious.

BETH: This is a light lunch, Viola. We'll probably talk more than we'll eat....

VIOLA: Oh I'm used to that. Theatre people always fuss with their food. I suppose it's because it's hard to act with food in your mouth.

BETH: I'll just have the Caesar Salad.

VIOLA: Dressing on the side?

BETH: Why do you say that?

VIOLA: Because most New York restaurants are like New York women. They overdress.

BETH: On the side, then, please.

VIOLA: *(To GARY)* And you, sir?

GARY: I want something light. Do you have any minestrone soup?

VIOLA: We do, we definitely do.

GARY: I'll have a bowl of that, please....

VIOLA: I know why.

GARY: Oh you do, do you?

VIOLA: Your stomach is acting up.

GARY: Actually it is, Viola. Because I am in the process of refusing what could be a very lucrative deal.

VIOLA: Aren't you glad I brought the bubbly?

GARY: I am, I am.

VIOLA: That's it then?

BETH: That's it.

VIOLA: *(Starts off, then stops)* Oh. *(To BETH)* You were asking about Gurney.

BETH: Yes? And?

VIOLA: I just called my boyfriend about him. The one who teaches? He said that Gurney may well be the most under-rated playwright in these United States.

GARY: Thanks, Viola.

VIOLA: With the possible exception of Shelby Feinstein.

BETH: Who's Shelby Feinstein?

VIOLA: *(Turning to go)* See? Same as Gurney...

GARY: Thanks, Viola.

VIOLA: You're more than welcome. *(She goes)*

BETH: Did you pay her to say those things?

GARY: I did not.

BETH: "May well be..." That's the most weasly phrase in the English language. May well NOT be, too.

GARY: We're not getting anywhere.

BETH: Just answer one question.

GARY: Depends what it is.

BETH: This play, does it have a political theme?

GARY: All good plays have political themes.

BETH: Yes, but is this one specifically political? On contemporary issues?

GARY: *(After a pause)* Very.

BETH: O K. Fine. Now the bottom line. Is this play about Bush?

GARY: Bush is no longer contemporary.

BETH: Still. Is it?

GARY: No more questions.

BETH: You should know there may be a considerable amount of money involved.

GARY: O K. Yes. The play is about Bush.

BETH: George W Bush? Not George Herbert Walker Bush. But young George W? It's about him?

GARY: Yes.

BETH: Even though he's left office?

GARY: Even be*cause* he's left office.

BETH: Even though it's all water over the dam, and blood under the bridge and all that?

GARY: Even because of all that.

BETH: Hmmm. *(Pause)* Let me be frank Is this play Gurney's attempt to give Bush the *coup de grace*?

GARY: *Coup de grace*?

BETH: Is it sort of a... what? A mercy killing?.

GARY: You could look at it that way.

BETH: Then this is the play my client definitely wants, and is very much willing to pay for. *(Reaches into her bag)* I have the contract right here.

GARY: Your client is a Bush-hater, isn't he?

BETH: A good lawyer does not comment on the motives of her clients.

GARY: But he is! Of course he is! I get it now! Your client is some rabid, far right, gun-toting Texas nut-case who is pissed off at Bush for what he's done to the Republican Party.

BETH: My client would prefer to be described as a concerned American.

GARY: O.K., OK., but however we describe him, your Texas client wants this play in order to publically humiliate Bush in his own back yard!

(VIOLA *comes on with their food)*

VIOLA: Soup's on! (Serves BETH)) Ladies first. Caesar Salad! ...An dressing. . *(Serves* GARY) And one bowl of delicious minestrone...crackers on the side... Mmmm yummy. *(She goes off.)*

BETH: Gary, let me say...

(VIOLA returns.)

VIOLA: *(Serving)* Fresh bread...nice and chewy in the ciabatta tradition... And butter, of course, for them that wants it...*voila,* from Viola.

BETH: Thank you, Viola.

(VIOLA stands and waits.)

BETH: I said, thank you, Viola.

VIOLA: You're talking about Bush, aren't you?

GARY: How'd you guess?

VIOLA: I heard you halfway across the room.

BETH: Oh Lord. I apologize. We'll try to keep it down.

VIOLA: Bush is responsible for where we are today, you know.

BETH: *(Dryly)* Oh really?

VIOLA: Wars in Iraq and Afghanistan, global warming, floods and hurricanes, it all comes back to Bush.

BETH: We are trying to get some work done, Viola.

VIOLA: And the economic meltdown. People seduced into buying homes, then cruelly evicted from them. If it weren't for Bush, this restaurant would be packed at lunchtime and this table would have been reserved over a week ago.

GARY: You go, girl!

VIOLA: If it weren't for Bush, this whole country would be on a roll. The rich would be poorer, the poor would be richer. Our movies would be good, our music better, and American theatre would be the envy of the world!

If it weren't for Bush, yours truly might be performing
a major part in a good new play right around the
corner, instead of spouting a few lame lines before
exiting to the kitchen. If it weren't for Bush. *(She goes off.)*

BETH: That's called scape-goating.

GARY: That's called an audition.

BETH: Well, we were talking about money.

GARY: Were we?

BETH: I was about to show you how much my
concerned Texan is willing to pay.

GARY: Go ahead.

BETH: *(Taking out a pad and a pen, writing a number on the
pan, ripping off the piece of paper)* My client...is prepared...
to offer this.

*(BETH slides the paper across the table to him. GARY takes it,
reads it, sends it back.)*

GARY: I see your client is hardly the huge fan you said
he was.

BETH: Not enough?

GARY: Not half enough.

BETH: My client is willing to negotiate.... *(Crosses out the
first figure, writes another, slides the paper back to him.)*

GARY: *(Reading)* Better. *(Sends it back)* But still below the
mark...

BETH: For an unfinished play? About a retired
ex-president?

GARY: To be optioned by an unknown amateur? From
Texas?

BETH: All RIGHT! *(Writes a considerably larger number on the paper, slides it back to him)* How amateur is that, may I ask..

GARY: Jesus H Christ!

BETH: Watch your language, please. We take religion seriously in Texas.

GARY: And money, too, I see. *(He looks carefully at the piece of paper)* Let me ponder this.

BETH: Ponder away. *(Pause. She watches him.)* Does Gurney have a family?

GARY: He does.

BETH: Children? Grandchildren?

GARY: Four children, eight grandchildren...

BETH: That's disgusting.

GARY: And he's not even Catholic.

BETH: I imagine those grandchildren will need help on their college educations

GARY: They already do.

BETH: I also imagine that the William Morris Agency needs reminding that the non-musical theater can occasionally bring in a substantial income.

GARY: I'm fast discovering that.

BETH: And finally, I imagine that you yourself could use the sizeable agent's commission to enhance the material side of your personal life.

GARY: True. My Mastercard's totally maxed out.. *(Looking at advance)* Your guy must hate Bush very much.

BETH: No comment. *(Reaching into her briefcase)* Here's the contract.... *(Hands him the contract)* It's fairly standard.

GARY: *(Taking it; opening his backpack)* I'll go over it in the silence of my lonely sublet.

BETH: Go over it now.

GARY: Now? Here?

BETH: Let's get this deal done today, Gary. Check it out, and then messenger it over to Gurney for his signature.

GARY: What's the big hurry?

BETH: My client is an impatient man.

GARY: I've heard that about Texans. Shoot first, ask questions later.

BETH: The point is I'm very much hoping to fly back to Houston later today with a signed contract in my hand—and a handsome check in yours.

GARY: I'm reading, I'm reading.. *(He reads.)*

(VIOLA returns.)

VIOLA: Food O K?

BETH: Fine, Viola..

VIOLA: I see you've introduced props into your scene..

BETH: Props?

VIOLA: *(Indicating)* Those pieces of paper you're pushing around. They may seem like just paper but they carry a tremendous amount of stage weight.

BETH: *(Dryly)* How interesting...

VIOLA: *(Indicating GARY)* For example, what he's reading now. That thick document. It looks major.

GARY: *(Looking up from his reading)* It is, Viola. Major.

VIOLA: *(To* BETH*)* I'm fascinated by how well you both handle what we call "stage business."

BETH: We are handling *private* business, Viola.

VIOLA: Whatever it is, it looks fascinating. Especially if it ties into your discussion of Bush. *(She goes.)*

BETH: That waitress is driving me mad.

GARY: Consider her comic relief..

BETH: Next thing you know, she'll want to sit down and join our discussions.

GARY: You asked on the phone for an informal restaurant.

BETH: Because I wanted to do business at the table. So let's do it..

GARY: Certainly. *(Thumbing through contract)* Most of this is standard boiler plate.

BETH: Nothing wrong with that.

GARY: I agree. I note that the substantial sum you offered is to be considered an advance against royalties.

BETH: Naturally...

GARY: Which gives your client sole rights to produce Gurney's play....

BETH: Yes. Of course.

GARY: I see no mention here of any particular theatre.

BETH: We have many theatres in Texas. In Houston alone, we have the Alley Theater, the Houston Rep, the Houston Astrodome

GARY: *(Shuffling through the contract)* Uh-oh.

BETH: What now?

GARY: I don't see any time frame here. Your clients want sole control of the material for how long?

BETH: Oh well. Quite a while, obviously..

GARY: Eighteen months? Two years? How long before the rights revert back to Gurney?

BETH: I believe, somewhere in paragraph seven, there is a reference to a time period.

GARY: Oh. *(Finding it, reading it)* I see the word "Open-ended."

BETH: That's it.

GARY: Open-ended.? Your Lone Star god-of-vengeance wants an unlimited amount of time to produce Gurney's play?

BETH: Which would give Gurney plenty of time to find his ending.

GARY: Ending or no ending, this contract allows your clients to hold onto the play forever. Without ever producing a line of it. What if he simply sits on it?

BETH: Why would he, with an advance as big as that?

GARY: How can I ask Gurney to sign a contract which ties up his play indefinitely? What do I tell him?

BETH: Tell him to go on faith..

GARY: Oh I see. This is a faith-based contract from Texas.

BETH: All right, yes.

GARY: All right, no. An unlimited option with an unknown producer? Sorry. This is slightly insulting.

(GARY tosses the contract back to BETH.)

BETH: *(Indicating the paper with the advance on it)* That is hardly an insulting amount of money. For a first draft of an unfinished play? Which the playwright himself might never even finish?

GARY: The advance would still hold?

BETH: Of course the advance would still hold. It's written into the contract. *(Handing back the contract, pointing)* Paragraph eleven.

GARY: *(Finding it, reading)* O K... So?

BETH: *(Takes out cell phone)* So at least call Gurney. Tell him the offer. Take my cell.

GARY: I have my own. *(Getting up, starting to dial, then stopping)* Nope. Can't do it. How do I know you don't represent some gang of crypto-fascist Texas weirdos who are out to nail Bush for all the wrong reasons? At least give me your client's name.

BETH: No..

GARY: Hey, it's only fair. I admitted the play was about Bush. You can at least ante up the name of your producer.

BETH: I can't.

GARY: *(Starting out))* Then I'm history.... *(He goes.)*

BETH: *(Calling after him)* Wait!

(GARY comes back on)

BETH: Jim.

GARY: His name is Jim?

BETH: Jim.

GARY: There's a Jim Simpson who runs the Flea Theater in Tribeca. He's done some Gurney plays, but he's not a Texan.

BETH: It's not that Jim..

GARY: What's his last name? This Jim?

BETH: I don't have to—

GARY: Yes you do. *(Standing up)*

BETH: O K! His name is Jim *(Mumble)* ... *(She slurs the second word.)*

GARY: Say again.

BETH: Jim *(Mumble)*.

GARY: I'm sorry. I still didn't get the last name.

BETH: *(Reluctantly pronouncing it more clearly)* Jim Baker...

GARY: Baker?

BETH: That's it.

GARY: Jim Baker, from Houston, Texas? ...Hmmm... Jim Baker...James...*Baker! James Baker, the Third, of Houston Texas* ?

BETH: I'm sure there are many James Bakers.

GARY: But are we talking about the distinguished Houston lawyer? The erstwhile Chief of Staff and Secretary of the Treasury under Ronald Reagan ? The Secretary of State under the first Bush Administration?

BETH: Possibly, yes.

GARY: We are talking about the consiglieri of the Bush family?

BETH: You may be.

GARY: Oh boy oh boy oh boy!

BETH: What?

GARY: I've just learned something.

BETH: Oh you have, have you?

GARY: Yes! I have just learned that you are not representing some angry and resentful Texas gunslinger, out to destroy Bush.

BETH: I'm not?

GARY: No, ma'am. You are representing the Bush family.

BETH: I'm not at liberty to—

GARY: The Bush family asked Baker to send someone up to New York to cut a deal with Gurney, and Baker sent you.

BETH: All right, yes.

GARY: Sent you to cut a deal which will make sure that Gurney's play—which they've heard is a dark and dangerous diatribe—will never see the light of day!

BETH: Yes, yes, yes!

GARY: All of which leads to several other questions.

BETH: *(Exhausted)* Such as?

GARY: How the hell did the Bushes hear about this play?

BETH: I told you. There's a lot of gossip in the theater....

GARY: I don't believe you, Beth! I doubt if there's much theatre talk bandied about the men's locker room at the Houston Tennis and Golf Club.

BETH: Then they must have heard about it elsewhere.

GARY: Elsewhere? An incomplete draft of an unproduced play? Written by a relatively minor author, under-rated though he may be?

BETH: All right! If you must know, there's an assistant in the theatre department at the William Morris Agency who heard you talking to your colleagues about this new play of Gurney's.

GARY: Yes? And?

BETH: *(Furtively) And because subordinates in the Morris theater department are badly underpaid, this assistant also does temp work for the C I A.*

GARY: Go on.

BETH: And at the C I A, she happened to be assigned to a rogue element which has remained profoundly loyal to the Bush family.

GARY: So this intern described the play to the C I A, who informed the Bush family.

BETH: Yes!

GARY: O K. Now another question. Why *you*?

BETH: Me?

GARY: Why did Baker send an inexperienced lawyer, just starting out.

BETH: Oh that's easy. Deniability.

GARY: What?

BETH: He wanted deniability. If the press got wind of any of this, Jim Baker could simply say I was an inexperienced female paralegal, and a loose cannon....

GARY: I must say I respect your honesty.

BETH: Thank you.

GARY: *(Getting up, pacing around)* But God, what a jerk I am! What a bone-head! I've been totally on the wrong track! I thought you wanted the play to attack Bush. Now I know you want to save his ass. Hey, you know what you've been really trying to do here, Beth?

BETH: *(Sarcastically)* No, what? Tell me

GARY: You've been trying to perform an abortion!

BETH: Oh please...

GARY: You've been attempting to snatch a play from the womb of its creator and crush out its life before it comes to term! Now I personally am passionately pro-choice. But this! This, from Texas! This, from a state aggressively committed to the right to life! This, from a woman who probably claims to respect the gestational process, even as she attempts to terminate it! I am thoroughly disgusted with you, and James Baker, and the entire Bush family!

(VIOLA *comes on.*)

VIOLA: You folks done?

GARY: I certainly am. I can't speak for Beth here.

BETH: I'm done, too.

GARY: She's been *un*done, Viola

BETH: True enough. I'm finished. I'm through.

VIOLA: Then I'll take your plates. *(Starts clearing off)* I hope there was nothing wrong with the food..

BETH: Nothing at all.

VIOLA: You didn't eat very much.

BETH: We asked for a light lunch..

GARY: But we got into something very heavy, Viola.

VIOLA: I won't probe any further. There are times when silence speaks louder than words, especially in the theatre. *(She clears silently.)*

GARY: *(To* BETH*)* Go back to Houston and tell the Bushes, "Mission definitely NOT accomplished."

BETH: Oh I will. And the next day I'll find a pink slip from James Baker taped to my computer monitor, dispensing with my services..

GARY: Don't be discouraged. Maybe you'll also get a polite thank you note from Barbara Bush.

VIOLA: I can't help but notice that you folks are still on the Bushes.

GARY: Are we ever.

VIOLA: I wish I could be party to your discussions.

BETH: Our discussions are over, Viola. You can bring the check.

GARY: *(To BETH)* I assume the Bush family will reimburse you for the full amount.

VIOLA: Don't be too sure. Read Bush's proposals on Medicare... *(She goes)*

GARY: *(Picking up his back pack)* Beth.

BETH: What?

GARY: Before I go, just a few more questions.

BETH: I've answered too many already.

GARY: These require a simple yes or no....

BETH: Oh well. We who are about to die say shoot.

GARY: Were you aware of what you were doing when you invited me to lunch?

BETH: Yes.

GARY: t your mission was to prevent, by whatever means possible, a new play by A R Gurney from ever being published, produced, or performed?

BETH: Yes.

GARY: Were you also aware that your whole approach was sly and deceitful from the start? Your ostensibly casual phone call to the William Morris Agency suggesting a light lunch. Your totally false assertion that your mysterious client was quote a huge fan unquote. Were you aware all along that you were using sly and dishonest means to stifle the legitimate utterances of a senior American playwright whose best works may well be behind him?

BETH: Yes.

GARY: Now the big question. And then I'm outa here....

BETH: Shoot.

GARY: Why?

BETH: Why?

GARY: Why the hell did you do this?

BETH: That requires more than a yes or no.

GARY: I'm waiting.

BETH: Bush has taken enough of a beating recently.

GARY: Oh yes?

BETH: All those humiliating cartoons in the papers. All those smart-ass skits on T V. All these recent tell-all books. And now that stupid Oliver Stone movie. I felt enough was enough. Besides, the anti-Bush criticism is becoming worse now he's out of office. Now the whole country is ready and eager to pile on the poor man. Take that Viola, for example. You heard her. All our troubles are all Bush's fault.

GARY: He called himself the Decider, didn't he? He stood there in the Oval Office thumping his chest like some silverback gorilla.

BETH: Yes well now, it's all too much.... Just last week there was a national poll which voted him the worst President in American history.

GARY: I read that.

BETH: So, think how the man feels, Gary. He can't turn on the television without some comedian making another crack. He can't pick up a newspaper without reading the latest analysis of his intellectual limitations. And now he's home, his mail is now inundated with threatening letters from bankrupt hedge fund managers..

GARY: Does he ever go out?

BETH: Very rarely. It's too dangerous.... Most of the time he simply wanders around that so-called ranch, taking half-hearted swipes with his chain saw at scrub oaks, and hiding liquor bottles from Laura.

GARY: Wow.

BETH: Yes, wow, Gary. Wow. What can the man do with the rest of his life. He talked about being baseball commissioner but now knows he'd be booed out every ball park in the country.

GARY: He could do some public service.

BETH: Republicans don't do that, Gary. Only Democrats, like Carter or Gore....

GARY: True.

BETH: All he can do is play golf, Gary. And he's no good at that. He's trapped into inactivity. So maybe now you can understand why his concerned parents would prefer not to see him publicly humiliated any further in some dumb play.

GARY: Hell, Beth. A play's just a play. Plays don't cause much of a splash these days, especially outside of New York.

BETH: Oh yes? Try googling Gurney some time. You'll see that many of his plays, because of their simple sets, and small casts, and tame ideas, are done by schools and colleges and amateur groups all across the country...

GARY: Hmmm. You're right.

BETH: The Bush family doesn't want that, Gary. So they asked Jim Baker wants to nip this play in the bud.

GARY: At least now you're admitting it.

BETH: I am. And I'm glad I am. And if I had the chance, I'd do it again.

GARY: Shit, Beth! This really pisses me off.! When I first saw you today, sitting at this table, waiting to have a light lunch, I have to tell you I was pleasantly surprised. I couldn't help but notice you were a very good-looking woman in roughly my own age bracket.

BETH: Thank you for that.

GARY: And as our conversation continued, we seemed— repeat, seemed—to be getting along famously.

BETH: That's true.

GARY: In fact, I'll even admit—deal or no deal—that after we finished lunch I was secretly hoping to invite you back to my apartment—which is conveniently located nearby, by the way—so we could indulge in some easy, non-committal sexual activity before you hopped on your plane back to Texas.

BETH: Oh Gary.

GARY: I'm serious! But now all bets are hereby off! I see you simply as a devious and manipulative closet Republican, who is probably intimately acquainted with Sarah Palin. Ugh. Oh God, what a corrupt and despicable world we live in. A bright and beautiful woman, with a potentially distinguished future in the law, lies, cheats, and almost steals, for in the hope of being promoted to partner in a corrupt Texas firm.

BETH: Oh please, Gary. Give me a break!

GARY: Sorry. I'm gone. (Starting out) Good luck in your future mergers and acquisitions, Beth! Or should I say murders and inquisitions!

BETH: Wait, Gary. Please.

GARY: Why should I?

BETH: Because I want to tell you something.

GARY: Such as?

BETH: That I'm also attracted to you.

GARY: Oh sure, oh sure.

BETH: It's true. Oh I know you're kind of a jerk at times, and any guy as connected with the theater as you are probably has gay issues on the side.

GARY: Hey, stop right there..

BETH: But still, you should know this: if you had invited me back to your apartment, I may well have agreed to go.

GARY: "May well have..." Someone once told me that was a weasly expression? *(Again he goes.)*

BETH: *(Calling after him)* O K, fine. Walk out on a woman just because she trying to salvage the ego of a former President of the United States. Walk out on a woman just because she believes in not hitting a man when he's down.

GARY: *(Coming back)* Say that again

BETH: The whole speech?

GARY: No, just the last part....

BETH: I don't believe in hitting a man when he's down.

GARY: I am suddenly amazed.

BETH: Why?

GARY: Because I recently heard Gurney say exactly the same thing..

BETH: He did?

GARY: About his play.

BETH: Really?

GARY: That's why he was having such trouble finishing it. He said that every time he tried to end it—these were his exact words—he felt he was hitting Bush when he was down.

BETH: You mean he didn't *want* to end it?.

GARY: He couldn't do it. He said that every time he looked at the fucking thing, he felt like a first-class shit..

BETH: He used that kind of language?

GARY: He did, and he normally doesn't.

BETH: I am impressed.

GARY: He also went on to point out that when Herbert Hoover was out of office, they left him alone. Same with Nixon or Gerald Ford. Who was he, A R Gurney, to pile on George W Bush?

BETH: This puts an entirely different light on things.

GARY: It sure does.

BETH: This explains why you were considering accepting my huge advance. You knew that Gurney had already abandoned the attack, so you might as well take the money and run...

GARY: Correct... Which means we're both rotten to the core.

BETH: *(Getting up)* It also means I can grab an earlier plane back to Texas. I'll tell Jim Baker and the Bushes that all bets are off. And it hasn't cost them a red-state cent except for my travel expenses and lunch. Maybe I won't get immediately promoted, but I'll still have taken a step up in my push toward full partnership.

GARY: I hope so, Beth.

BETH: And the really good news is that George W Bush can enjoy his retirement from public life without enduring the slings and arrows that Gurney hoped to hurl in his direction. *(Signals off)* Now where is Viola with that check?

GARY: Hold it.

BETH: What?

GARY: Gurney hasn't actually abandoned the play.

BETH: No?

GARY: In fact, he's begun the process of rewriting it from top to bottom.

BETH: Are you serious?

GARY: I am. He's obsessed with Bush. So he's now developing an entirely different slant on the guy....

BETH: What kind of slant?

GARY: A very positive slant.

BETH: How do you know?

GARY: Because I've already seen a draft of what he's up to.

BETH: Why didn't you tell me?

GARY: I couldn't. I promised Gurney I wouldn't mention his conversion to a soul. He's worried he'll lose his many liberal friends.

BETH: But you're mentioning it now.

GARY: Only because sometimes a good agent has to take matters into his own hands. Now that I know you and Gurney are on roughly the same page, maybe we can still do business.

BETH: Same page?

GARY: You both want to redeem the guy.

(VIOLA enters with the check.)

VIOLA: Enter server, carrying check.

BETH: *(Sitting down)* We've changed our minds, Viola. We'd like to see the dessert menus.

VIOLA: That's exactly why I've been delaying my entrance. I've been watching you two. I could tell by your blocking that your scene was taking a different turn.

GARY: Our plot is thickening, Viola.

VIOLA: Good. I love twists.

BETH: So how about those dessert menus?

VIOLA: Immediately. *(She goes.)*

BETH: "Quickly", as they say in interviews on T V, tell me what you know about Gurney's revisions.

GARY: I can't do it quickly.

BETH: At least has he found his ending?

GARY: Not yet, but he told me he's moving relentlessly toward a powerful one..

BETH: This is amazing.

GARY: Yes it is. And from what have I seen of his new draft, I'd say the play is almost ready to go public.

BETH: And you say the play is kind to Bush?

GARY: Beyond kind. Some critics might ultimately call it laudatory.

BETH: And the play itself is good? As a play, I mean. It's not just another piece of propaganda?

GARY: The play is sensational.

BETH: Of course you said that about the earlier draft.

GARY: This one is even better.

BETH: So says his agent.

GARY: Yes. But in this case, his agent feels the play is so good it's ready to be workshopped.

BETH: Ready to be what?

GARY: Given a workshop production..

BETH: And what in heaven's name is that?

(VIOLA *returns with dessert menus.*)

VIOLA: The dessert menus. *(To* GARY*)* I took the liberty of attaching my head-shot and resume to yours.

GARY: *(Looking at head-shot)* Quite the star..

VIOLA: Thanks.

GARY: I used to peddle these things around myself.

VIOLA: You did?

GARY: Oh sure. I started off as an actor.

BETH: I didn't know that.

GARY: Now you do. *(To* VIOLA*)* Nice resume. Interesting credits.

VIOLA: From what I have overheard of your conversation, you might want to notice that I have played Saint Joan.

GARY: In a regional theatre?

VIOLA: No, in junior high school. When we read it in class..

GARY: *(To* BETH*)* See? Resumes can be deceiving. She's squeezing in an amateur credit.

VIOL:A Only because of my passionate interest in political theatre.

GARY: Tell me this, Viola. Do you know what a workshop is?

VIOLA: Of course.

GARY: Would you describe one for Beth here?

VIOLA: Gladly. *(To* BETH*)* Workshops happen all the time in the theatre. Very few plays are simply written. Most are re-written, after going through some kind of a workshop. It's a developmental process, with a director, actors, and sometimes a few minimal pieces of scenery.

BETH: Are there critics? Are there reviews?

VIOLA: There are not. Just a few invited friends in the audience. To cheer you on and wish you luck. Oh I love workshops.

GARY: How about the cost, Viola?

VIOLA: Oh well, they cost money. To rent the space. And pay he actors..

GARY: To pay everyone except the playwright. But are they worth it, Viola?

VIOLA: Oh yes. Because they prove once again, as the theatre always does, that the whole is greater than the sum of its parts.

GARY: *(To* BETH*)* There you are. That's a workshop.

BETH: And that's what Gurney wants?

GARY: That's what Gurney's *agent* wants. Because Gurney is no spring chicken. This play may be his last gasp, and he needs a workshop to get it right.

BETH: I wish him luck.

GARY: As a matter of fact, Gurney's agent is beginning to think...

BETH: Think what?

GARY: ...that it would be a cool idea to take the advance offered by James Baker and apply that money to a workshop of Gurney's play....

BETH: Gurney's agent is being silly.

GARY: Gurney's agent is being serious.

VIOLA: May I add something here?

BETH: No. *(Turning to the menu)* I'll have the fruit cup, please, Viola....

GARY: *(Checking menu)* And I'll try the Tiramasu.

VIOLA: About that workshop. I'm available and interested.

BETH: How lucky we are.

VIOLA: I could play a bereaved widow from the war in Iraq. Or a disgruntled Katrina victim. Or an evicted home-owner in an unemployment line.

BETH: Did you get our dessert orders, Viola? I didn't see you write them down?

VIOLA: Oh I can remember them.. I'm a quick study. Which you have to be if you're in a workshop.

GARY: What would you think, Viola, of a play that attempts to redeem George W Bush?

VIOLA: It must be a terrible play.

BETH: So you wouldn't be in a workshop?

VIOLA: Sure I would. It's a job. *(She goes.)*

(Pause)

GARY: So.

VIOLA: So?

GARY: Is Baker's offer still on the table?

BETH: You are seriously asking the Bush family to pay for Gurney's play?

GARY: As Gurney's agent, I'm hereby proposing it as an excellent deal for both sides. Gurney gets the chance to work out the kinks in his plot, the Bush family gets the chance to see George's reputation sweetly restored.

BETH: Oh for God's sake.

GARY: Why not, Beth? The Bushes wanted to buy off a derogatory play. Why shouldn't they subsidize a complimentary one?

BETH: How do I know it's complimentary?

GARY: Because, event from a cursory reading, I can absolutely guarantee that in this play, George W Bush turns out not to be the ass-hole everyone thinks he is.

BETH: *(Dryly)* Oh goodie. May I quote you to James Baker?

GARY: Sure. As long as you add that Gurney's play hopes to rehabilitate George W Bush in the eyes of his country and the world.

(VIOLA comes back, with the desserts on a tray.)

VIOLA: Here we are.

BETH: Thank you, Viola.

VIOLA: Anyone want coffee?

BETH: No thanks.

VIOLA: Looks like you're both wide awake without it.

GARY: Beth here is toying with the idea of funding a workshop of Gurney's play.

BETH: Beth is not.

VIOLA: Do it, Beth!

BETH: Bring the bill, Viola.

VIOLA: Of course. *(She goes.)*

BETH: All right now. I'm going to say something positive here.

GARY: It's about time.

BETH: I'm going to admit that, in a strange way, I'm slightly tempted by this workshop idea.

GARY: You are?

BETH: If I can come back to Texas with a complimentary...with a complimentary...

GARY: Call it a "salute" ...

BETH: ...All right, if I can come home with a complimentary salute to George W Bush tucked under my arm, why it would...

GARY: It would help your career immeasurably..

BETH: Yes, dammit, it might. And it would certainly help the poor Bush family, currently cowering in Kennebunkport....

GARY: No question.

BETH: Of course if I did commit Bush funds to this workshop thing, the source of their investment would have to be kept....

GARY: Strictly secret. I totally understand.

BETH: Otherwise it might seem...it might seem...

GARY: ...what we call in the theatre a vanity enterprise.

BETH: All right then. Tell you what. I'll take the play and read it on the plane before I decide. Please call Gurney and have him messenger a script over to this restaurant..

GARY: He won't allow anyone to read it.

BETH: How can I possibly ask James Baker to invest money in a work which I haven't even read?

GARY: Because I'm about to tell you about it. I'll call on my expertise as an enthusiastic agent, a competent

ex-actor and a natural story teller to fill you in. Then
you can fly back to Houston top-heavy with talking
points.

BETH: Oh Lord. I'm on the fence here.

GARY: I do admit that for this narrative process to work,
I'll have to count on a certain collaborative spirit from
you.

BETH: I'm willing to try.

(VIOLA *comes on, no longer wearing her apron.*)

VIOLA: Your revised bill

BETH: *(Taking the bill)* Thank you, Viola. *(Noticing her)*
What happened to your apron?

VIOLA: The manager said I could take a brief
mid-afternoon break

BETH: I see.

GARY: Viola, before you take it, could you to make a
further revision in the bill?

VIOLA: Gladly.

GARY: We'd like to order two glasses of that delicious
Pinot Grigio you mentioned during the exposition....

BETH: *(To GARY)* Why wine?

GARY: Because it will help you to willingly suspend
your disbelief.. *(To VIOLA)* Viola, I am trying to sell this
lovely lady on Gurney's play, and I have the sense that
she needs a little juicing up.

BETH: *(Handing VIOLA her credit card)* Bring the wine,
adjust the bill, and then you're free, Viola.

VIOLA: May I stay? I'm desperate to hear about this
play.

BETH: Oh I don't think...

VIOLA: A play that redeems Bush? I can't walk away from that..

GARY: Get the wine and join the party.

BETH: This is a private lunch, Gary.

GARY: Yes , but we're dealing with public issues.

VIOLA: I'll get the wine. *(She goes.)*

BETH: She'll interrupt constantly.

GARY: That's all right. You can tell Baker that Gurney's play converted even a Bush-bashing waitress.

BETH: Well, start your talking points.

GARY: *(Handing her a pad and pen from his briefcase)* Let me give you a few preliminaries before Viola comes back.

BETH: *(Writing)* Preliminaries.

GARY: Gurney told me that once he started rewriting his play, he came to realize he personally had a great deal in common with George W Bush.

BETH: *(Looking up)* In common? With Bush?

GARY: He actually admitted it. He said they both came from large, close families. They both were brought up in what people call a privileged life.

BETH: Which means?

GARY: Which means that both went to private boys boarding schools, and reputable New England colleges, and expensive Ivy League graduate schools. In other words, both had what was once considered the finest education money could buy.

BETH: *(Writing)* Fellow WASPs

GARY: Strike the word WASP. Gurney hates it. He thinks it's pejorative, inaccurate, and reductive.

BETH: *(Crossing it out)* It doesn't work for Bush anyway. He's more a simple country boy from Midland Texas.

GARY: No. Gurney says that's just a pretense... Droppin' his consonants at the end of his words, wearin' jeans and cowboy boots, and playin' John Wayne on the international stage. Underneath all that, Gurney and Bush belong to the same cultural community and share the same desire to grow beyond it.

BETH: *(Writing)* Cultural community. *(To* GARY*)* I wish you'd amplify that....

GARY: I'll try. Gurney says over the years there have been certain incidents or events which have enabled his own family to feel a kind of kinship with the Bushes. It's almost as if the two families were signaling to each other across the moiling, messy tumult of American democracy....

BETH: Go on.

GARY: O K. For example, one of Gurney's uncles once danced with Bush's aunts at her coming-out party in Greenwich in the late nineteen-fifties.

BETH: *(As she writes)* Coming-out party...Greenwich... the fifties....

GARY: And a cousin's of Gurney's wife once rode up on the double chairlift at Stowe with Bush's niece during Christmas vacation.

BETH: Chairlift...Stowe...Christmas vacation

GARY: And Gurney's sister's grandson has recently become involved with Bush's sister's husband's step-daughter in Hobe Sound, Florida. They might even get married if they can work out their respective trust funds in a pre-nuptial agreement.

BETH: Hobe Sound...prenuptial...

GARY: So you see that in all these examples there is a certain amount of cultural cross-fertilization taking place.

BETH: I suppose.

GARY: This naturally makes A R Gurney feel a tribal compatibility with George W Bush.

BETH: *(Writing)* Tribal compatibility.

GARY: But Gurney's identification with Bush goes even farther than that.

BETH: Even farther?

GARY: Both are the eldest sons of affable fathers and non-nonsense mothers. Both, over the years, have found themselves overburdened with heavy paternal expectations. Both have made a concerted effort to avoid being simply carbon copies of their attractive but domineering dads.

BETH: "Attractive". I love that word, "attractive".

GARY: That word is another cultural signal in and of itself.

BETH: I sensed that....

GARY: In any case, both sons, to avoid simply duplicating their fathers, struck off in new directions. For example, in his youth, young George challenged Bush Senior by getting drunk, driving recklessly, and doing dope.

BETH: All right, all right.

GARY: While young Gurney thoroughly disappointed his father by dating women who chewed gum and getting kicked off the varsity squash team for smoking one lousy Chesterfield..

BETH: *(As she writes)* This is becoming weirdly fascinating.

GARY: So because he understands Bush so well, Gurney is now trying to do two things. First, to resuscitate the reputation of the forty-third President of the United States...

BETH: *(Writing)* "Resuscitate the reputation" That's good.

GARY: And two, Gurney is hoping to redeem WASP values at a time when they're considered shallow, useless and obsolete.

BETH: *(Writing)* "redeem WASP..." *(Crosses it out)* No. I won't bother with that. It's not important. *(Looks at her notes)* But I have to say some of your other points are quite persuasive.

GARY: At least they explain why Gurney is obsessed with George W. Bush, and desperate to give him a fair shake. In a strange way, Gurney is trying to rehabilitate himSELF..

BETH: Know what? I'm almost tempted to call Jim Baker right now and tell him what we're up to....

GARY: Not yet. Now it's time to give you a bigger picture.

(VIOLA comes in with three glasses of white wine on a tray.)

VIOLA: Pinot Grigio coming up. *(Handing a glass to BETH)* For you. *(To GARY)* For you. *(Settling in at the table)* And for me.

BETH: I take it you've decided to join us.

VIOLA: I have. And I put my wine on your bill. You can consider it my tip.

BETH: *(Dryly)* That's very thoughtful, Viola. *(Signs bill, retrieves credit card)*

GARY: Are we ready, then, to move forward with my attempt to sell Gurney's play.

BETH: Go ahead.

VIOLA: *(Joining them at the table)* I'm with you.

GARY: It begins, as you may guess, with a magnificent scene between father and son.

VIOLA: Oh I love magnificent scenes!

GARY: The Father is congratulating his son on his election to the presidency, and gently pointing out that it was an extremely close election where the son actually lost the popular vote.

VIOLA: Ouch. Don't remind me.

GARY: Poppy Bush goes on to say that James Baker had to do some serious finagling in Florida and some arm-twisting at the Supreme Court to get the kid to win.

VIOLA: How terribly, terribly true!

BETH: I'll skip that part when I describe the play to Baker.

GARY: The point is, it's a touching scene. The father urges the son to tread carefully, avoid partisanship, and work for the benefit of the country as a whole.

VIOLA: Right on!

GARY: And then Poppy goes on to advise young George on the selection of his cabinet ...Do you mind if I stand up here? I can tell it better when I'm on my feet.

VIOLA: Of course.

BETH: Go right ahead.

GARY: *(Standing up, as Bush Senior)* Steer clear of Cheney and Rumsfeld , the father says. They worked for me and I know them well. They'll want to run the ship, but don't you let 'em...

VIOLA: Does the Father say why?

GARY: Because they're shits, he says. Rumsfeld, he says, is a smug little shit,, strutting his stuff in front of the press corps like the riflery instructor at some second-rate summer camp....

BETH: Wow. That's strong stuff.

GARY: And Papa Bush goes on to say.... *(As Bush senior)* "Beware also of Cheney and his whole gang of draft-dodging neo-cons. They sit around much too much and never get enough exercise. Which is why they're drooling to send our boys off to war.

VIOLA: Beautiful!

BETH: Baker may say that's too much..

GARY: Ah, but that's what workshops are for. Tell him the dialogue is negotiable. Gurney may be willing to rewrite.

VIOLA: He could say they were "rascals". Instead of "shits"....

GARY: See, Beth? We're in already workshop mode. An actor is making valid suggestions

BETH: May we move on, please? What does young George say in response to his father?

GARY: Ah hah! Here's the point of the scene. Young George says nothing.

BETH: Nothing?

GARY: Not a word.

VIOLA: Silence can be extremely powerful on stage. Remember? I pointed that out in some earlier dialogue...

BETH: Go on, please.

GARY: He waits until his father leaves, and then turns to the audience and gives this brilliant, quasi-

Shakespearean soliloquy. I'm not who you think I am,
Dad, he says. I'm not your pet puppy, Poppy.

VIOLA: Wow!

GARY: In fact, he says, I intend to appoint the very guys
you advised me not to.

VIOLA: Oh my God! What a speech that must be!

BETH: But why? Does he give a reason?

GARY: He does. He wants his father to realize he's
finally come into his own. He's at last shaking off all
the heavy Bush baggage he's been carrying on his back
for fifty years. So his father calls him on the telephone.
(As papa Bush) Georgie... *(As George W)* Call me
Mister President, Dad. *(As papa)* Mister President...
I thoroughly disagree with your appointments. *(As
George W)* Tought titty, Dad. *(As papa)* I'm serious, son.
At least bring in someone like Brent Scowcroft or James
Baker, just to leaven the lump?

BETH: *(Writing)* Baker will like that.

GARY: *(As himself)* But Bush hangs up on him.

VIOLA: What? Hangs UP? On his own father?

BETH: So Gurney makes the Bush father-son
relationship a Freudian thing.

GARY: He does. Because he understands it personally.

VIOLA: At least Gurney didn't go into Iraq when his
father begged him not to.

GARY: No, but Gurney went into the theatre when his
father begged him not to.

VIOLA: Same thing, same thing. Both are dangerous
enterprises, where things can go terribly, terribly wrong.

GARY: Good point, Viola. *(To BETH)* See? This girl is
good.

VIOLA: The whole thing is sort of like Greek tragedy, isn't it? These two men—Bush and Gurney—challenging their gods by trying to assert their own identity.

BETH: *(Dryly)* Very good, Viola.

VIOLA: My boy-friend teaches tragedy at the New School.

BETH: Tragedy or not, I'm nervous about selling this to Baker. He may like the references to himself, and the compliments Gurney pays to George Bush Senior, but so far the play hardly redeems young George W.

GARY: Now wait. That's just how the play begins. Gurney has him grow from that point on.

BETH: *(Taking up her notebook again)* Tell me how.

GARY: Well ... now I'm improvising here a little, because I only read the play once...but after the cruel and useless war in the Iraq, and the inexcusable response to Hurricane Katrina, and the ghastly horrors of Abu Ghraib, and of course the economic recession...

BETH: Hold it. The play goes into all that stuff?

GARY: Gurney is a master at compression. But here's the thing. At the end of his second term, Bush is holding his final press conference, and a reporter asks him how he feels about his Presidency, and Bush replies, "Oh fine."

VIOLA: Just. "Oh fine"?

GARY: That's exactly what the reporter says, "Oh fine, Mister President? With the world fast falling apart all around you, and you just feel fine?" And Bush stares at him for a moment, petulantly.

VIOLA: Petulantly. Perfect...for Bush..

GARY: And here comes the twist. Gurney writes a stage direction: "Bush's face changes." And he says, "Oh well, mistakes were made".

BETH: "Mistakes were made"? That's all?

GARY: But don't you see? Bush has never before even mentioned mistakes. And so the White House press corps starts muttering "Rudabaga rudabaga."

BETH: Rutabaga, rutabaga?

VIOLA: *(To* BETH*)* That's what crowds always murmur on stage. Let's show her.

GARY & VIOLA: *(Acting it out)* Rutabaga Rutabaga

BETH: All right. I get it, I get it!.

GARY: But then a young female reporter raises her hand and says, "But Msiter President, you recently said you were the Decider!"

VIOLA: I'll do the reporter. "Mr. President, you recently said you were decider."

GARY: *(As Bush)* "Did I say that, Winkie?"

VIOLA: *(As Winkie)* "Yes you did, Mister President."

BETH: Winkie? Her name is Winkie?

GARY: Bush gives her that name.

VIOLA: I want to play Winkie in the workshop.

GARY: So Bush says, " O K, Winkie, sweetheart, I may well have made a few mistakes."

BETH: What? He admits it? He uses the active voice?

GARY: He says he may WELL have made them. Which, as we know, is cop-out. And here Gurney writes a crucial stage direction for the actor playing Bush: "A faint glimmer of guilt crosses the President's face."

VIOLA: He doesn't smirk at all?

GARY: He does not. And there's no sly chuckle either....

BETH: So that's how the play ends? With this faint
glimmer of guilt?

GARY: Not at all, Beth! Jesus! Give me a break! The play
is far more profound than that. Gurney immediately
adds another stage direction. He has Bush turn away
from the podium. *(He acts this out.)* And walk up the
wide red carpet behind him, back into the bowels of the
White House. Only this time he doesn't strut. And his
elbows aren't sticking out, so he doesn't look as if he
were holding a porcupine under each arm. No sir, he
just kind of shuffles away, stooped and pensive, as if
he were actually beginning to think things over....

VIOLA: Beautiful! You're a good actor, Gary.

GARY: Thank you, Viola.

BETH: And a good agent, Gary.

GARY: Thank you, Beth.

BETH: But I'll be frank with you, Gary. Nothing you've
told me so far could possibly persuade James Baker to
fund a workshop for this play.

GARY: Wait, wait, dear lady! Have another sip of white
wine.

VIOLA: May I get you some more?

BETH: No thank you, Viola.

GARY: I'm just showing how Gurney leads us toward
a new and changed George W Bush. Bush goes much
farther than that. And so does Gurney.

(VIOLA looks off, gets up.)

VIOLA: Would you excuse me a minute?

GARY: Sure.

VIOLA: Don't tell any more till I get back.

GARY: O K. I won't

VIOLA: *(Picking up the empty wine glasses)* I'll take these off your hands.

BETH: Thank you.

VIOLA: And bring more.

GARY: Please do

VIOLA: I may also bring a surprise for you. *(She goes.)*

BETH: I still don't like her.

GARY: She's a good audience. And a good actor.

BETH: You just like preaching to the choir. *(Looking off)* She's got something up her sleeve. I feel it in my bones.

GARY: Do you feel anything else in your bones?

BETH: Excuse me?

GARY: Such as feelings for me, now that I'm seizing the ball and running with it?

BETH: No comment.

GARY: Because my feeling s for you have returned.

BETH: Really?

GARY: Yes. I feel I'm reaching you in a new way. I have the sense that you're opening up to my earlier proposition....

BETH: Not so fast thee, buster.

(VIOLA returns with a tray of four white wine glasses)

VIOLA: Here we go.... *(Putting a glass in front of BETH)* For you, Beth... May I call you Beth?

BETH: If you have to.

VIOLA: *(Putting a glass in front of GARY)* And for you, Gary...

GARY: Thanks.

VIOLA: *(Puts a glass at her place)* And for me, Viola...
(Puts a glass at an empty place) And for Marshall.

BETH: Marshall?

VIOLA: Remember I told you I had a boyfriend who
teaches drama?

BETH: Yes. And?

VIOLA: That's my surprise. He's here.

BETH: Here? Now?

VIOLA: He sometimes stops by to wish me well on
his way to his class at the New School....

BETH: How sweet.

VIOLA: He wants to join us.

BETH: Oh please.

VIOLA: His specialty is tragedy. He feels he can
contribute something to our discussion.

BETH: Oh Lord.

VIOLA: *(She beckons off)* Come on, Marshall.

*(MARSHALL comes on. He's possibly a little older than
the others.)*

MARSHALL: Hiya. guys..

VIOLA: *(To MARSHALL, indicating)* Beth... And Gary.

MARSHALL: Hi Beth and Gary

BETH & GARY: Hi Marshall.

MARSHALL: *(Settling at the table)* I guess you might call
me a *deus ex machina.*

BETH: A what?

MARSHALL: It's a Latin expression. For a Greek dramaturgical device. Translated literally, it means the god from the machine. When things got complicated in a Greek play, they would use a kind of mechanical crane to lower the actor playing a god or goddess onto the stage. This new figure would adjudicate the events of the play and provide some sort of a solution to its various problems.

VIOLA: Isn't he marvelous?

MARSHALL: Viola here has told me that you're discussing a play on Bush by Gurney...

GARY: That's right.

MARSHALL: Let me say that I'm a huge fan of Gurney's work. Huge.

BETH: I've already used those lines.

GARY: *(Raising his glass)* Nonetheless, welcome, Marshall.!

(They all drink)

GARY: Now what we're trying to do, Marshall, is persuade the lovely Beth here to convince the Bush family lawyer James Baker, that they should fund a workshop of a play which redeems George.

VIOLA: I told him all that.

MARSHALL: I will say that what sounds compelling about Gurney's play is that it seems to be asking a fundamental and essential question.

GARY: About George W Bush?

MARSHALL: Not just about Bush, Gary. Gurney is bigger than that. His play would seem to be asking an essential question about American democracy—or any democracy, for that matter.

VIOLA: Tell them what it is, Marshall.

MARSHALL: I'm trying to do just that, sweet heart.
(To others) The question is, whether an elected political
official, whether President or dog-catcher, is ultimately
accountable for the damage he may have done.

GARY: I like that.

MARSHALL: Gurney is trying to write about
accountability.

BETH: Accountability. That sounds interesting.

MARSHALL: Never say anything is interesting in
the theatre, Beth. Never. It's the kiss of death. Why?
Because "interesting" describes only an intellectual
experience. Plays should always invoke an emotional
response. They should be exciting, fascinating, or
compelling.

BETH: I'll try to remember that.

MARSHALL: Let me say something else on this point.
In our democracy, our leaders are quick to be
celebrated for the good they have done, or what they
think is the good they have done. They are eager to have
buildings and airports and bridges named after them,
sometimes even when they are still alive.

VIOLA: How true. The Ronald Reagan airport,
MacArthur Park, the Kennedy Center. I could go on
and on.

MARSHALL: But don't, sweetheart. The point is we go
along with all that because they are responsible for
bringing some good into the world. But what about
the politicians who mess things up? Aren't they
responsible, too? How do we deal with them?

BETH: I don't know.

MARSHALL: Well, from what Viola has already told me,
I'd say that's what Gurney is trying to do in his play.

GARY: There you are.

MARSHALL: Gurney's Bush would seem to be struggling to accept his own complicity in the damage he has done at home and abroad. Now that very struggle is something to be celebrated. It's what makes Greek tragedy so special, and Greek democracy so vital. The Greek tragic heroes, such as Oedipus or Ajax or Electra, may have done harm to their communities but in the end they acknowledge the damage they have done. They assume responsibility, take it onto their own shoulders, and because there is no ultimate or superior system of justice to punish them, they go on to punish them*selves* for their errors..

BETH: Hey. I like this.

MARSHALL: And by punishing themselves, these tragic heroes—or heroines—purge the world of the corruption they have caused.... And only then can the human community begin to recover its pride and confidence.

GARY: Makes sense to me.

MARSHALL: Now, Gary: does George Bush do this in Gurney's play?

GARY: Punish himself? He tries.

MARSHALL: Even though Bush may have done what he did with good intentions, he still takes the blame when it turns out to be wrong?

GARY: That's what Gurney wants him to do.

MARSHALL: And the community—not Thebes or Argos now—but rather the American community, if not the rest of the world—becomes a cleaner, purer, better place as a result of Bush's action?

GARY: We can only hope.

VIOLA: This is totally fascinating.

GARY: *(To* BETH*)* Surely Baker would fund a play that did that.

BETH: I have to admit I'm impressed. *(Indicating her notebook)* But I need to take back to Texas a few more specifics in order to make it convincing....

GARY: Of course. Now we left George W Bush with a look of anxiety on his face. So Gurney gives us a new scene where he visits his father, He says he feels this "terrible ache." Or words to that effect. He has noticed that the world is in a major mess, our country's reputation is in the cellar, and he feels somewhat responsible for it.

MARSHALL: Somewhat? "Somewhat" is not a tragic word..

GARY: I'm not finished. He says he feels somewhat responsible, and his father replies, "That's because you made a major mistake."

VIOLA: By causing a war?

GARY: "No...by admitting your guilt" his father says. "That's something a politician should never, never do! And there's only one thing you can do to repair the damage."

BETH: And what's that?

GARY: Write a note.

MARSHALL: Write a NOTE?

GARY: Like a sympathy note, or a thank you note.

MARSHALL: That's all?

GARY: Poppy Bush says that's what he did after his trip to Tokyo in 1989 when he barfed into the lap of the Premier of Japan.

BETH: I remember that.

GARY: Well, he apologized in a personal note. He tells his son to do the same thing..

BETH: *(To* VIOLA*)* That's a Wasp thing. Writing notes.

VIOLA: I know that. I'm not that dumb..

GARY: So that's what Bush does in Gurney's play. He gets a piece of the presidential writing paper which he swiped from the White House when he left office. And he locates a pen which still uses liquid ink. And after several drafts, he completes a note of apology to the American people, saying he feels some responsibility for the way things are. He expresses his deepest sympathy for those who may have suffered, and he's terribly sorry about it.

VIOLA: But who does he sends the note *to*?

GARY: *The New York Times* and *Vanity Fair.*

VIOLA: And they publish it?

GARY: Immediately. And *The Times* even adds a photograph the letter, so their readers can see the misspellings and recognize its authenticity.

BETH: This is kind of amazing.

GARY: And the letter is translated into many different languages, including Arabic, and people write columns and articles about it, and John Stewart makes jokes about it, and it makes generally quite a splash.

BETH: I should think it would.

GARY: But there's a problem with it.

BETH: A problem?

GARY & VIOLA: *(Together)* It doesn't work....

MARSHALL: I could have told you that. You may have noticed I've been silent. That's simply because I 'm

appalled by the inadequacy of the gesture. It's not
tragic at all.

GARY: O K, but the big thing about Bush is that he
realizes that, too!

VIOLA: He does?

GARY: He does. So he immediately does something
more. He wangles a guest spot on the *David Letterman
Show*

VIOLA: I love David Letterman!

MARSHALL: This is possibly a step in the right direction.

BETH: T V's good. At least it's a public medium.

GARY: So Bush shows up with his entourage of Secret
Service, which spreads out backstage and in the
audience, and then David announces him and he comes
on stage.

VIOLA: Does the studio audience boo him?

GARY: No. They're actually kind of polite. But you can
tell they're unhappy with him.

MARSHALL: Like one of those muttering choruses in
Euripides.

GARY: Right. So Bush soldiers on. He shakes hands with
Letterman, settles into his chair, and crosses his legs,
and after a few introductory jokes from David, he
speaks. "Seriously, David," Bush says, "I do want to
acknowledge some of the terrible things that happened
during my administration." Something like that.

VIOLA: He "acknowledges?" That's a big word.

GARY: He was speaking from notes.

VIOLA: But that's all he said?

GARY: No, no. He takes it one step further. He says that
he feels "more than somewhat responsible" for the

mess that the world is in. He goes on to admit that these things happened "on my watch" and he feels "considerable regret."

VIOLA: Yes! He's becoming responsible!

GARY: He is.

BETH: An ex-President of the United States! Admitting his guilt on nationwide T V!

GARY: And whose words are immediately broadcast, by satellite, all over the world.

VIOLA: And does that do it? Does it make our country feel better about itself, and does the rest of the world begin to forgive us?

GARY: No.

BETH: No? Then where does Gurney take him from there?

GARY: He doesn't.

BETH: He doesn't?

GARY: That's where Gurney stops.

MARSHALL: He ends his play *there*?

GARY: He doesn't call it an ending.. He just stops, with Bush standing alone on stage, in a spotlight, facing the audience, while over the sound system we hear his apology translated into many different languages, echoing all over the world, as the light on him dims slowly to darkness,

BETH: I like it.

VIOLA: So do I.

MARSHALL: I don't.

GARY: Neither does Gurney. Has Bush learned anything? Has the world forgiven him? We don't know. Gurney himself calls it a Truffaut-esque ending.

VIOLA: A what ending?

GARY: Truffaut-esque. After the great French film director. Because it evokes the ending of *The 400 Blows*, where we fade out on the young hero, standing on a beach, the sea behind him, the world closing in on him, as he stares hopelessly out at the camera.

VIOLA: What's wrong with that?

GARY: Gurney feels it's a cop out.

VIOLA: I think it's fascinating. *(To* MARSHALL*)* Don't you, Marshall?

MARSHALL: I hate it.

VIOLA: Oh dear.

MARSHALL: No wonder Gurney is dissatisfied with it. It makes him guilty of everything he accuses Bush of being.... He leaves his play hanging—just the way Bush left his country...

BETH: But what else can Bush do?

MARSHALL: Something more, and something major, if he is to redeem himself and the world.

VIOLA: You mean like those Greek heroes, sweetie?

MARSHALL: Precisely. Or like many of those other heroes who follow bravely in the tragic tradition. Hamlet. Othello. Even Willy Loman. They all take big steps at the end.

VIOLA: You mean they kill themselves.

MARSHALL: Yes, they do, Viola, if we're going to be frank about it. And because they do, their communities are purged and purified as a result..

BETH: So you're saying Gurney has to kill Bush.

MARSHALL: I'm saying that's a definite possibility.

GARY: *(To* BETH*)* See, Beth? See why a workshop is
so essential. Even here, in this restaurant, over a light
lunch, we're already working to help Gurney arrive
at a more fulfilling conclusion.

BETH: Well I'm sorry. I refuse to fund a workshop
where Gurney murders Bush. I veto that right now.

GARY: I can tell you this, Beth. Gurney yearns for some
sense of purgation in our country. He keeps mentioning
his eight grandchildren and wishing he could write a
play that would make the world a better place to grow
up in.

VIOLA: We all want that.

BETH: But what can he do that he hasn't done?

GARY: Are we talking about Gurney or Bush?

MARSHALL: Both. May I take over here?

BETH: Be my guest.

VIOLA: *(Giving him a quick kiss)* My deus ex machina.

MARSHALL: Let me say that what we're really looking
for here is a recognition scene.

BETH: A recognition scene?

MARSHALL: What Aristotle calls an *anagnorisis.* Where
the hero makes a crucial discovery about his true
situation.

GARY: Yes. O K.

MARSHALL: O K. Now what Gurney has given us
already is several partial recognitions.

BETH: Go on.

MARSHALL: The feelings of guilt. The Letterman admission. In all these scenes, Bush partially realizes what he has done, and partially apologizes. But he still feels unfulfilled and we, the human community, still harbor feelings of deep resentment and disappointment..

GARY: Right.

MARSHALL: Now let me say that there is nothing intrinsically wrong with partial recognitions. I'm afraid partiality is the condition of modern life.

BETH: How true.

VIOLA: Howtrue.

MARSHALL: On the other hand, this is a play about George W Bush, a still-young man who was born with far more advantages than most.

VIOLA: I'll say.

MARSHALL: Naturally we have the right to expect far more of him in the long run, do we not, Beth?

BETH: We do, we do.

MARSHALL: And for the same reasons, we have the right to expect more of Gurney, too.

GARY: Oh yes. Absolutely.

MARSHALL: So somehow Gurney's got to give Bush real stature. For example, if this were an Elizabethan play, he could have him fall on his sword.

VIOLA: Does Bush own a sword? Anyone know?

MARSHALL: Even if he does, and happened to fall on it, that would be an outmoded alternative.

VIOLA: He could shoot himself then. He must have a gun on his ranch. To kill rabbits or something....

MARSHALL: Guns don't seem right for Bush. Cheney maybe. But not Bush.

BETH: So what are you proposing?

MARSHALL: You mentioned a movie, Gary. A film by the French director Francois Truffaut. I propose that Gurney consider a more appropriate film, and a more American one.

VIOLA: Which movie, sweetie??

MARSHALL: David Lean's filmic masterpiece *The Bridge On The River Kwai.*

GARY: But David Lean is English.

MARSHALL: The film was written by an American, produced by an American, and contains several American stars.

BETH: It sure is one of my favorite films.

MARSHALL: That may be because it contains once of the great recognition scenes in Twentieth Century drama.

GARY: Are you thinking of the Colonel played by Alec Guinness?

MARSHALL: I am indeed. Toward the end of the film, Guinness suddenly confronts William Holden who has come to blow up the bridge that Guinness has so lovingly built as a proud example of Western expertise and knowledge.... *(He begins to act this out.)* "You!" Guinness says to Holden Then he looks at his beautiful bridge just as a train full of Japanese soldiers is about to cross it and extend their occupation of Southeast Asia. And he suddenly recognizes that by building this magnificent bridge he has only given aid and comfort to the enemy. So Guinness gasps and says, in horror, "What have I done?"

VIOLA: *(Acting it)* What have I done?

GARY: It's like our invasion of Iraq, which has given aid and comfort to Al Qaida..

MARSHALL: Hold it. I'm getting there. So then Guinness is hit by a hail of bullets, and staggering sideways, he falls onto the plunger of the dynamite device to blow up the bridge.

BETH: I got it on Netflix. And the troop train falls into the river, and the Japanese advance is prevented.

MARSHALL: Right. Now the question is, did Alec Guinness totally recognize his error and try to rectify it? Did he purposefully and heroically destroy his own handiwork?

ALL THE OTHERS: We'll never know.

MARSHALL: But we do know this: he becomes a far bigger man at the end. He becomes a man we admire because he says, "what have I done?" and he falls on the plunger. So we forgive his past delusions, and the war ends, and the world is at peace, and Guinness gets an Academy Award.

BETH: Wow.

MARSHALL: See? Partial recognition and ambiguous death. That's what we want from Bush. Do you agree, Gary?

GARY: I do, I do.

VIOLA: That's my man.

GARY: Yeah, but could you give us an idea of how that might work in Gurney's play.

MARSHALL: Certainly. Now remember I'm winging it here, but suppose Gurney has former President Bush fly to Iraq on what is described in the press as a personal, post-election, fact-finding tour. " I want to see first-hand what we accomplished on my watch," he reads from his teleprompter. So he flies to Baghdad first-class on Saudi Airlines, and stays in the Green Zone. He inspects the mammoth fortress of our embassy still under construction, and drives by our frightening, monolithic prison for terrorists, and stops briefly at our military hospital where he chats with those few soldiers whose wounds don't require immediate evacuation.

BETH: Hold it.

MARSHALL: Yes, Beth?

BETH: Can you show all that in a workshop?

VIOLA: The theatre is an imaginative medium, Beth.

GARY: Gurney can call for special lights, sound effects, and maybe even slide projections.

VIOLA: *(Indicating* MARSHALL*)* And remember: a good actor can evoke an entire world in one speech.

MARSHALL: Thank you, sweetie... May I continue, Beth?

BETH: Go ahead.

MARSHALL: Bushis so pleased with what he sees, these lucky soldiers and these imposing buildings, that he asks to be taken out of the Green Zone for a view of Baghdad and beyond. And so, sitting in his armor-plated HumVee, driving through the pre-arranged clusters of Iraqis stationed on either side, and peering through his thick security guard, he is shocked by what he sees.

GARY: The devastated buildings and abandoned houses.. The reeking pools of untreated sewage. The flickering lights in the empty shops, the damaged mosques, and indeed whole neighborhoods of rubble and debris.

MARSHALL: No.

GARY: No?

BETH: But you said Bush was shocked.

MARSHALL: He is. What shocks Bush is what he sees in people's eyes.

BETH: People's eyes?

MARSHALL: The eyes of the Iraqi people. He expected cheers and the light of freedom shining in their faces. But he sees nothing but grim resentment and sullen anger and sad disillusionment. He also notices these qualities even in the faces of our own men guarding him. And he is also reminded of the expressions he has seen on faces back home,. And he glances back over his shoulder at the barbed wire of Green Zone, and our great, hulking edifices constructed to remain there forever—and he says quietly to himself, what does he say, Beth?

BETH: He says, "What have I done?"

MARSHALL: Exactly! "What have I done?" So there's your partial recognition, Gary. But by now his entourage is moving on, and up ahead he sees another cluster of Iraqis. "Are those Shiites or Sunnis or Al Qaidas?" asks our ex-president. The General beside him says it's hard to tell. Ah, but within this group he sees one individual who is actually smiling and waving a small, torn American flag. "There! You see?" Bush says. "I want to shake that man's hand! I want to shake the hand of freedom." "I wouldn't, sir, " the General says. "It's still dangerous out there." "Freedom is always dangerous," says Bush, and he steps out of his vehicle, brushes aside his security guard and walks slowly toward the cluster of Iraqi citizens, and the tiny, torn flag fluttering feebly in their midst. Then suddenly shots ring out and from all sides there is a hail of bullets —from the street, from the rooftops, from Bush's military security escort, and in the confusion—

GARY: He staggers and falls.

VIOLA: Like Alec Guinness.

GARY: Is he killed?

MARSHALL: He is.... By resentful Shiites. Or by angry Sunnis. Or possibly even by friendly fire.

BETH: Accidentally on purpose.

GARY: You could say he asked for it.

MARSHALL: You see? An ambiguous death.

VIOLA: What an ending!

MARSHALL: And to bring down curtain, you might suggest to Gurney that he have the Mormon Tabernacle Choir singing the Frank Sinatra song, *I did it My Way.*

VIOLA: Look at me. I'm crying. These are real tears. I swear..

MARSHALL: That's because you're feeling a real catharsis.

BETH: A what?

MARSHALL: Aristotle again. A feeling of purgation, which comes after you've felt pity and terror.

GARY: Pity and terror...

MARSHALL: Pity for Bush and what happened to him. And terror that his gross neglect of basic human principles could easily happen to you and me, were we in positions of power.

VIOLA: That's exactly what I felt, Marshall.... A catharsis in spades.

MARSHALL: And so , subliminally, we become better citizens.

BETH: I am totally torn here.

GARY: *(Getting up)* You know what, Marshall?

MARSHALL: What?

GARY: I have a strong urge to call Gurney and tell him your idea.

MARSHALL: Be my guest.

GARY: I want to lay it on him while it's still fresh in my mind.

MARSHALL: *(Reaching into his pocket)* Of course. Use my cell.

GARY: *(Taking out his cell)* I've got my own.

BETH: You can call right here.... Don't mind us.

GARY: No, Beth... If Gurney senses that I am calling from a restaurant, he'd hang up immediately.... Restaurants, he says, are communal places like theaters, and cell phones violate their essential integrity. I'll find some isolated place to make my call. *(He goes.)*

VIOLA: *(To* MARSHALL*)* Well done, sweetheart.

MARSHALL: Thanks.

VIOLA: *(To* BETH*)* Do you think James Baker will buy it?

BETH: I doubt it.

VIOLA: Or the Bush family.

BETH: Definitely not..

VIOLA: But it's so moving. And it redeems Bush big time..

MARSHALL: *Partially* redeems him, sweetheart.

VIOLA: It turns him into a tragic hero, Beth....

BETH: Yes it does. But it kills him in the process.

MARSHALL: Let me say this, Beth. Endings are always hard. Especially for plays as profound and complicated as plays by Gurney. Now as I said earlier, a play about Cheney could easily end with a hunting accident. That would feel right and appropriate, wouldn't it?

BETH: Absolutely...

MARSHALL: Or if this were a a play about Donald Rumsfeld, Gurney could have him drown in his own swimming pool, to suggest the water-boarding he was ultimately responsible for.

VIOLA: *(To* GARY *and* BETH*)* Isn't he marvelous? You can see why I'm so madly in love with him.

MARSHALL: Or if this were a play about Condoleeza Rice....

VIOLA: She could enter a nunnery "chanting faint hymns at the cold and fruitless moon."

MARSHALL: Excellent, sweetheart!

VIOLA: I played in *Midsummer Night's Dream* in grammar school.

*(*GARY *comes back in, snapping shut his cellphone; they all look at him.)*

BETH: Well?

GARY: I told Gurney about our gathering here and he said that he was delighted to hear that the younger generation is so actively involved both in politics and in the theatre. He hopes you'll also take the reins in other areas of American life.

MARSHALL: "Take the reins." What a quaint old expression. It comes from an agrarian culture where horses predominated. But what about our ending?

GARY: Ah well, he didn't buy it.

MARSHALL: What?

VIOLA: Are you sure you told it right?

GARY: I sure tried to. But he said it seemed contrived and derivative.

MARSHALL: Derivative?

GARY: He said it reminded him too much of *The Bridge On The River Kwai.*

MARSHALL: That's the fucking POINT!

GARY: Well, he didn't like it.

BETH: And neither will James Baker.. *(Looking at her watch)* Maybe I can catch the early plane back to Houston *(Gets up)*

GARY: Hold it.

BETH: What now?

GARY: Gurney had another idea .

BETH: For an ending? For Heaven's sake, tell us.

VIOLA: The suspense is killing me.

GARY: Gurney thinks the Bushes should end the play themselves.

BETH: What?

GARY: *(To* BETH*)* He wants you to give the play to the Bush family so they can work out their own ending,

BETH: What?

GARY: Gurney says that the Bush family is ultimately responsible for Dub-ya, and they should deal with him as they see fit.... *(He goes to his backpack.)*

BETH: I don't have the play.

GARY: I do. *(Fishing in his backpack, hands her a script)* Here.

MARSHALL: *(To* VIOLA*)* This is what the Greeks called a peripetea, or sudden turn of events.

BETH: *(To* GARY*; as she thumbs through it)* Why didn't you show this to me before?

GARY: Because Gurney asked me not to show it to anyone....

BETH: What changed his mind?

GARY: He's abandoning it to work on something else.

BETH: How does Gurney think the Bushes family will respond?

GARY: Gurney says that's a problem. They might just ground him for a week or so. Or cut down on his allowance.

VIOLA: I'll bet they burn the manuscript immediately.

MARSHALL: Good! That would give it a Wagnerian ending—the Twilight of the Bushes....

BETH: *(Putting the script in her briefcase)* May I tell James Baker that the Bushes have an unlimited option to do whatever they want with this thing?

GARY: Absolutely.

BETH: And what will it cost?

GARY: Not a nickel. It's on the house. I'll bet Jim Baker gives you an immediate promotion.

BETH: If I want it.

GARY: You mean you don't?

BETH: I'm learning to like New York. Including you, Viola.

VIOLA: Likewise, I'm sure.

BETH: Goodbye, Marshall.

MARSHALL: Goodbye, Beth.

BETH: As for you, Gary...

(BETH *takes* GARY *aside; they hug)*

BETH: I may come back next week..

GARY: Let's do lunch again.

BETH: Good. Let's start there. *(She goes.)*

VIOLA: *(Calling after her)* I'll put fresh flowers on the table! *(Looks off)* Uh oh. There's the manager. I have to set up for the evening..

MARSHALL: *(Helping her clear off)* And I'd better get to the New School for my course on theatre criticism.

GARY: What's your theme?

MARSHALL: The same as Gurney's. Namely that we're all—all—including critics—all in this thing together.

(They all start out. As they go:)

VIOLA: *(To GARY)* Did Gurney tell you what's he's doing next?

GARY: He's writing a musical.

VIOLA: Good choice.

GARY: About Barack Obama.

VIOLA: Oh my.

GARY: He's calling it "Hello, 'Bama.". He's even written a song for it.... *(Sings)* Hello, 'Bama ...well Hello, 'Bama:

VIOLA & GARY: *(Joining him)* "It's so nice to have you right where you belong."

VIOLA: Sounds like a hit.

MARSHALL: Sounds like plagiarism.

VIOLA: Tell Gurney to keep me in mind. I do a heavenly Hillary.

(They are all off by now.)

END OF PLAY